Copyright

A Girls Guide to Empowerment

By Jasmine Henderson

All rights reserved. No part of this publication may be reproduced, stored in a retrieval system, or transmitted in any form or by any means-electronic, mechanical, photocopy, recording or any other-except brief quotations in printed reviews, without prior permission of the publisher. Bible verses are taken from various translations of the Holy Bible.

Anointed Hands Publishing

Nina Motivates LLC

www.ninaaddison.com

publishernina@gmail.com

Cover photo

Photographer: Tony Sharp, Chicago IL .

Instagram: @subtlearray

Copyright© 2022, Nina Motivates LLC

All rights reserved to Jasmine Henderson

ISBN: 979-8-9864595-3-0

This Book Belongs To

_____

To: Mikeda Webb

Thank you for the opportunity. Without your consideration of me this book wouldn't have been possible. You get Webbs in motion.

Jason Henderson

Forward

Elizabeth's Mom has a passion for helping young women find their strength and power. Her experiences directing and choreographing a praise team; leading workshops on empowerment and being fully present for her own daughter and her friends has provided many opportunities for her skills to be developed into this book. It is simply written, but the questions challenge you to think about how you wish to live your life. I pray you chose to be empowered.

Elizabeth's Pastor – Pastor Carol Jameson Brown

Table of Content

A Girls Guide to Empowerment 5

What is Girl Empowerment? 8

Chapter 1: Self Awareness 11

Chapter 2: Positive Body Action, not Image! ... 16

Chapter 3: Peer Pressure VS. Peer Support 22

Chapter 4: The Importance of Me Time 26

Chapter 5: Pay It Forward 30

Chapter 6: Dream, Plan, Work, Earn 33

Chapter 7: Skills and Knowledge 36

Let's Wrap it Up! 40

Workbook 42

About The Author 55

Photo Credit 57

A Girls Guide to Empowerment

A Word from Mom

There are a lot of mediums out these days speaking on the empowerment of girls and women. These mediums range from t-shirts to posters to stem classes and organizations such as Girl Scouts and Girls on the Run. So, what's all the fuss about? From the day our girls come into the world they are bombarded with blatant and subliminal messages of who they are supposed to be and how they are supposed to look, how they are supposed to act. From the sexy Bratts and Monster High dolls, to the tv shows we watch and music that we listen to constantly reinforcing female sexuality. As hard as we may try as parents we live in a world where it is getting harder to shield our children from the world around them. A world that doesn't always have their best interests at heart. We may even be inadvertently sending our own messages inside the home. My mother dieted most of my childhood, even though I loved her curves, and couldn't wait to grow a few of my own; it felt normal to monitor and restrict food portions. I have an excellent mother, but what we needed was a conversation, and at the end of that conversation perhaps she would have realized she didn't need to diet any more than I did.

Empowerment posters, and t-shirts that say "You Go Girl" are all well and good, but we need to make sure we are keeping the conversation open with our young ladies. We need to continue to point out that the images they see aren't real. Point out the photoshop and the extensions. Teach them the sexual behavior in videos are not only fake, but the long-term damaging effects to one's self esteem; and in turn show them what healthy and natural looks like. It's not enough to tell them "You are a Queen." We need to ask them "How are you today?" We need them to check in not only with us but with themselves. We need to help them build confidence through their skills and be open to letting them try and build on new skills sets. We need to show them external sources of validation, such as boys, aren't the key to long term happiness. Studies show that girls who participate in activities that allow and encourage them to express themselves and their knowledge have higher self-esteem. We need to remind them to be wholly happy people as they define the type of person they want to be.

I hope this book addresses some of these issues, I hope it opens the conversation. I want girls to speak up for themselves about their feelings and express their strengths and victories. I want them to strategize how to hone their skills to build into their future. Most importantly I want them to support each other, and know that a victory for one of them is a victory for all.

For God has not given us a spirit of fear, but of power and of love and of a sound mind. 2 Timothy 1:7

Signed Jasmine Henderson

What is Girl Empowerment?

Girl Empowerment is really about choices and taking responsibility for those choices.

- You don't need anyone's permission to follow your dreams, as long as you are willing to do the work to achieve those dreams. If you want to be a doctor, or Business CEO, join the military, or stay at home and take care of a family, it is okay. Nobody can tell you that you can't do that. because It's your choice. That's empowerment.

- When you have the support of your friends and family and community to help you build your goals, that's empowerment.

- Valuing yourself and being valued by the people you care about, that's empowerment.

- Creating spaces, where we as girls are comfortable being ourselves and talking openly to each other about things that are important to us. That is empowerment.

- Being free to ask questions and gain knowledge about whatever interests you... That's empowerment.

Empowerment, in its simplest form, is when people have control over their own lives.

How can you help empower girls?

Chapter 1: Self Awareness

What is that?

Self-Awareness is knowing you, who you are. Not just your name and where you live. It's knowing what you like and don't like and being honest with yourself about your feelings. Sometimes we aren't honest with ourselves because we want to fit in with what everyone else is doing, or we want to make someone else happy.

Do you ever do something just to make your friends happy? What about mom or dad? Let me be clear if mom or dad say it's time to clean your room. You should do that because they are teaching you how to take care of yourself.

If Mom or dad wants you to learn to play the piano, but you feel like a drums kinda girl, don't play the piano to make them happy. Because you will be unhappy. SPEAK UP! Respectfully have a conversation. Let them know how hard you will work at learning the drums. Then actually work hard at the drums. You will be happy, and mom and dad will be happy you are being honestly YOU.

Sometimes Self Awareness means being Brave

Everybody wants to fit in. Sometimes when all your friends are doing something, you want to do it too, so you don't get left out.

For example...

What if your group of friends decides the group will only wear pink. But you don't like pink. You have never liked pink. Be honest with your friends. And if they don't understand that you are not into pink, then they are not your friends. That's ok. You can be brave and make new friends.

Sometimes when we are brave, it helps someone else be brave enough to be themselves too. Another friend may agree with you and say "Hey, I don't want to dress the same as you guys. I want to dress like me. "

Boundaries

Self-Awareness is very important for creating personal boundaries. Boundaries are the rules we set for ourselves and our relationships.

For example, if you know you are not comfortable hugging people you don't know, set a boundary. So when your parents introduce you to a new grown up and they try to hug you, tell them, "I'm not comfortable with that, but I will shake your hand."

Setting personal boundaries shows people you have respect for yourself, and it teaches people how to respect you, but don't forget to be respectful in return. It is not empowering to be rude.

Check in

Always be honest with yourself first. Second be honest with your friends and family.

- Ask yourself how does this really make me feel?
- Do I want to do this?
- Why? or why not?

Chapter 2: Positive Body Action, not Image!

What is that?

Having a positive body image is accepting your body the way it is and being comfortable with it. Even when some people tell you how **they** think a body should look. Because all bodies are made a little bit different. And our differences are what make us unique!

One way to communicate to other people how you feel about yourself is with body language. Do you hold your head down or up when you walk? Do you slouch? Do you try to make yourself as small as possible? Do you stand tall with your chin up? These are the ways we show how we feel about ourselves.

Don't let outside stuff change the inside!

There are a lot of things around us that try to tell us what our bodies "Should" look like.

- Maybe you see a lot of very pretty models on Instagram, or YouTube. Maybe you notice how the girls look on television shows. You must remember all those models, youtubers, and actors/actresses' job is to sell you something. They need you to want to be like them, so you will follow them, and buy their stuff, so they make more money. **They need you,** and just because you like them, does not mean you have to **be** just like them.

- I know sometimes you go clothes shopping, and it's hard to find clothes that fit you. That doesn't mean changing your body. It means you need a better store, with better options.

Them Problems Vs You Problems

- If television or social media is telling you, you need to change to be more like them, That's a **"them"** problem.
- If somebody else doesn't like the way you are shaped, that's a **"them"** problem
- If somebody doesn't like what you wear, **"them"** problem... (with an exception for parents. If your parents are uncomfortable with what you are wearing, say "let's have a conversation." Maybe they are trying to teach you something)
- If you aren't comfortable, that's a **"you"** problem

"Them" problems can go find themselves some business, but **you** problems need to be fixed; because you have to be happy with **YOU**!

Every Person's body is not for everybody...

- Just because your friend is shaped a certain way doesn't mean you should be too. You are not the same person. Let them be them, and you be you, because trying to look like somebody else is only going to stress you out. You were given your own body for a reason.

- We all have some things we don't like about ourselves. Do you feel too short? or too tall? Maybe you don't like your nose? Well, there is someone out there who wishes they had a nose just like yours. Don't focus on things you don't like. Focus on things that make you happy. **Think Actions not images!**

How do we support a girl that's doubting the way she looks?

■ Gas her up! Remind her why she's great. Remind her how smart, and funny, or creative she is. Remind her why you are friends. Remind her of all the people in her life who love her.

■ Remind her of the things that are important to her...

• What makes her happy? What gives her peace?

• What are her abilities? **Actions not images**!

How do I work on Having a Positive Body Action?

- Work on loving your Body for all that it can do!
- Focus on the Positive things that you know how to do. Or learn to do something new! Do things that boost your confidence.
- Don't compare yourself to images on social media, tv, or magazines. It's not real. #filtersbelike
- Catch negative thoughts about yourself and replace them with positive ones.
- Remember that you are a Whole Person with thoughts and feelings. You are Not Just Body Parts!
- Remember that you and your body are unique. Our differences build our style and personality. So Do You Boo!
- Hang out with people who love themselves and encourage you to love **You** too!

Check In

There is only one You, and you are beautifully made.

Is there something about you, you don't like?

How can you turn that answer into a positive thought?

Chapter 3: Peer Pressure VS. Peer Support

What is that?

- **Peer Pressure** is - When you feel like you must do something because everyone else is doing it

- **Peer Support** is - When you help your friends be the best "them" they can be.

What is the difference?

Peer **Pressure** makes you...
- Feel like you have to do something that you should not do.
- Do something you normally don't want to do. You don't want to feel bad afterwards.

Peer **Support** encourages you to...
- Do things that are good for you,
- Do things that would make you feel better
- Be the best authentic You

Let's play Scenarios

Scenario #1

A girl in your class is really shy and quiet and doesn't have many friends. She's really good at science and wants to enter the Science fair. But the rule is you must have a partner to enter. Even though you weren't interested in participating in the fair she asks you to be her partner. If you participate, Is it Peer Pressure or Peer Support?

Answer: It is Peer Support. Not only is this a great opportunity for both of you to learn something really interesting about science, but it's also an opportunity to make a new friend. Plus, you will be helping someone do something they love to do. Help her let her light shine!

Scenario #2

A popular kid at school is having a party, and your best friend wants to go because she wants to hang out with the popular kids and be popular too. You don't want to hang out with those kids, because they are rude and are always making fun of you. Your friend is afraid to go by herself and says she needs you to go with her. She tells you if you were really her friend you wouldn't let her go alone. Do you go to the party? Is it Peer pressure or Peer Support?

Answer: Its Peer Pressure. A real friend wouldn't try to make you hang out with people who would make fun of you.

A real friend would not want to be friends with those kids. Your best friend is not supporting you and your feelings. If that is who she wants to hang out with, she should go alone.

Scenario #3

You and your friend separately enter the Talent Show at school. The winner gets free tickets to the Water Park. Even though you are an awesome piano player, your friend is a very talented singer. She wins the tickets to the water park and asks you to come with her. You're a little mad you didn't win. Do you go? Is it Peer Pressure or Peer Support?

Answer: Peer Support. She wants to celebrate her win with you. So, guess what... You win too! You didn't get first place, but you get to have a lot of fun with your friend. And you are both still very talented.

But Why Tho?

Why do we have peer pressure?

Because nobody likes to do things by themselves. Let's pretend a bully is picking on a kid named Alfred. If the Bully can get everyone to pick on Alfred then nobody will tell the bully she is wrong. Because everyone is doing it. Then the bully doesn't have to feel bad about being mean and hurting Alfred's feelings. But it is wrong to be a bully. It takes a brave person to be kind to Alfred when others won't. Peer pressure is about creating a group mentality so that the bully or person adding the pressure doesn't feel alone.

You know another way to help someone not feel alone?

PEER SUPPORT!

Check In

Friends create **Support** not **Pressure**

Did you give in to Peer pressure Lately? What do you wish you had done differently?

Name a time you supported someone you care about?

Chapter 4: The Importance of Me Time

What is that?

Me time is taking some time in the day, or the week when you are doing something you enjoy by yourself. Usually, it is something that is relaxing for you, like reading a book or watching a tv show you like. It takes a lot of energy to be around people. Even if it is just your friends and family. Me time, is a time you get to recharge your personal battery.

Between school, family, chores, friends, after school activities, and homework, life can get very busy. Our

minds can get very crowded with thoughts and feelings. You can start to feel pretty stressed out! Sometimes you have to take a little time to yourself to clear out all of those extra thoughts.

Try to take a at least 5 minutes a day when you can be still, quiet, and alone. This is not the time to check your social media, or text your friends. The only thoughts you want to have are your own. You don't want to be influenced by anyone else's.

Suggestions for me time

- **Meditation** - is a great way to slow down. All you have to do is find a quiet place to sit. Close your eyes and slowly breathe in and out. Count while you breath. In 1,2,3,4,5. Out 1,2,3,4,5. Do that a couple of times, not thinking about anything but breathing.

- **Journaling** - Sometimes when you are thinking hard about something it helps to write your thoughts down. It's always nice to have a journal. A private notebook just to get your thoughts out so you can look at them. Try making a list of things that make you happy, and things that don't make you happy. Remember as you grow, those things can change. Because you are always changing. But as long as you are happy and comfortable with who you are. That is what's important.

It's not really important how you spend your "Me Time" as long as you spend it alone. You are learning to be confident in enjoying your own company. You can't always be with your friends or your family. You have to be able to be happy and comfortable when you are by yourself as well. It's also important to know when you need to take a break from people so you can "Check in" and see how you are feeling.

Check in

Close your eyes and take a deep Breath.

-What do you want to do when you finish reading this book?

Chapter 5: Pay It Forward

What is that?

Paying it forward is when you acknowledge that somebody helps or has helped you, so you help someone else.

Nobody does anything all by themselves, NOBODY. Everyone at some point has gotten help from someone. Being empowered is not just thinking about yourself. It's also about being a positive influence on the world around you. What is more empowering than helping someone in need?

"See a Need, Fill a Need"

There are hundreds of kids all over the country who have started their own business or charitable foundation because they saw an opportunity to help.

You don't have to start a business or charitable foundation. That takes a lot of time and money that you might not have right now. You can start small by.

- Helping with chores around the house without being told
- Picking up the trash in your neighborhood.
- Volunteering at a senior center or animal shelter
- Planting flowers to help the bee's
- Building bird feeders
- Join a volunteer program at your local library

There are so many ways to help others, and it feels good knowing you were able to help.

How awesome would this world be, if everyone pitched in and did at least one nice thing for someone else? Look around, how can you be of service?

Check In

"When we give cheerfully, and accept gratefully, everyone is blessed" - Maya Angelou

Who have you blessed?

Who can you bless?

Chapter 6: Dream, Plan, Work, Earn

What is That?

This Chapter is about setting goals. We may have an idea of what our goals look like. But we don't always know how to get there. Sometimes it helps to come up with a plan or a strategy. It's okay if that strategy changes. Sometimes while you are working on your plan, you learn some new information, and you have to change your plan a little. A goal can be anything. A toy you want to buy, a trip you want to go on, a job you want to have. No matter what it is, most goals take time and work, and with planning most goals are achievable.

How Do I Achieve my goals?

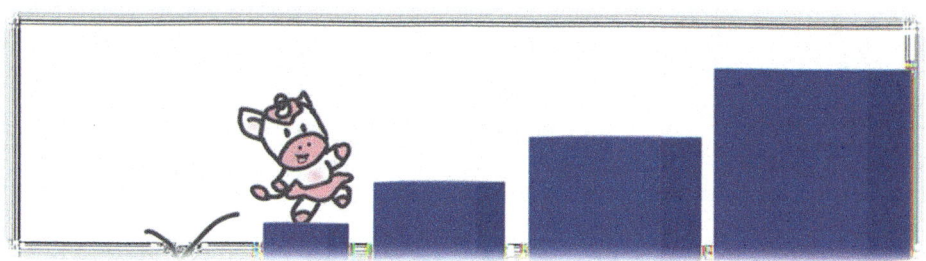

1. Break big goals into little goals.

For example, if your goal is to clean your room start with one corner. When that is clean, pick another corner. Stay in a small area until it is clean. When you accomplish little goals at a time the big goal isn't so big!

2. Focus on the short goals, they are steppingstones to the big goals.

It can feel discouraging when your goal is so far away. Like a job when you are a grown up. But if you focus on little goals, you can achieve those right now. For example, if you want to be a Vet, a short goal could be to volunteer for the animal shelter. Or read books about lots of different animals. And don't forget to get good grades at school. All those are important building blocks to build a future in helping animals.

3. Celebrate your success!

When you achieve a small goal don't forget to celebrate your hard work. Every step counts.

4. It's okay to change the plan a little.

Sometimes things don't go exactly the way we want. It's okay if we don't want that same goal anymore. You can change and work for something else.

5. Talk about your goals.

The more you say out loud what you want, the more likely you are to work hard for it. Also, the more likely other people will want to help you achieve your goals.

Check In
"One part at a time, one day at a time, we can accomplish any goal we set for ourselves." – Karen Casey.

Name something you have achieved recently.

_____

_____

_____

Chapter 7: Skills and Knowledge

What is That?

A Skill Set is a combination of knowledge, experience, and the ability to do something. As you grow and learn you will spend your life developing lots of different skills. Some examples of skills are

- How many words you can type on a keyboard without making a mistake
- Learning different kinds of dances
- How to cook
- How to sew or repair your clothes
- Speed reading
- Flips
- Drawing

- Doing large math problems in your head.

Sometimes skills come naturally, you just know how to do it. But 99% of the time they are something you decide to learn how to do. When you are an adult, having a skill is like having a tool you need to do a job. The more tools you own, not only the better you can do the job, but the more people will also pay you to do it.

Got Skills?

What is something that you know how to do? The more you practice things you know how to do the stronger your skill gets.

If you aren't sure you have any skills, think of something that is interesting to you, and then study it. Do you like video games? Study how they make video games! There are a lot of very easy coding programs for kids that can teach you how to make your own video game. Now all of a sudden you have a skill that you not only enjoy, but someone will pay you to use! All it takes is a little learning.

But you say, I'm not in school right now. I don't feel like learning. I hate to break it to you, but you will NEVER stop learning new things! Every day adults have to learn new things so they can accomplish the goals or do the work they need to do. And it's not easier just because you are a grown up.

The Learning never ends

Learning is what keeps your mind growing.
Some of you may have had a bad experience at school. So, you feel like learning is boring, but that just means the teacher was boring. Learning can be fun and interesting and is as necessary for life as food and water.

- So, find a subject that interests you and study it until you are an expert.
- Ask Questions wherever you go.
- Practice, practice, practice your skills

Check in

"The Ability to learn is a Skill, The willingness to Learn is a choice". - Brian Herbert

What was something that was hard to learn, but you did it. (Yay You!)

Let's Wrap it Up!

In this book I hope you have learned about the importance of

1. **Girl Empowerment** - The Freedom to make your own choices, and taking responsibility for those choices.

2. **Self-Awareness** - Knowing who you are inside and out, and understanding the things that make you comfortable, happy, and motivated.

3. **Positive Body Action** - Focusing on your abilities.

4. **Peer Support** - Positively lifting other people, and only hanging around people who lift you up.

5. **Me Time** - Taking time by yourself to recharge your battery.

6. **Paying it Forward** - Being helpful to others.

7. **Achieving Goals** - Writing a plan, using small goals to achieve big goals.

8. **And building Skills** - The more skills you can master, the more opportunities you will have.

Sometimes it can seem hard, or even unfair being a girl; but more than anything I want you to understand you are beautifully and wonderfully made. There is no one like you. You are all smart, and capable of achieving great things, if that is what you choose to do. Stay motivated, work hard, never lose sight of who you are, and if you have been blessed, be a blessing to someone else.

Workbook

Self-Awareness

1. I'm Happy when I _____

2. I'm Sad when I _____

3. I'm comfortable When _____

4. _____ Makes me uncomfortable.

5. I Love to _____

6. _____ Makes me feel safe.

7. _____ Makes me mad.

8. I Like to go to _____

9. I would like to learn to _____

10. Some of my favorite things are

    _____

    _____

11. _____ Is what makes

    me Unique

Positive Body Action, not Image!

1. What do you love about you?
   _____
   _____
   _____
   _____
   _____

2. How are you like your family?

   I got my _____ from my father

   I got my _____ from my mother

   I am _____ like my grandmother

   I am _____ like my grandmother

   I am _____ like my aunt

   I _____ like my cousins

You are more than a body. Use the letters to give positive words that describe the wonderful You that You are.

A _____

C _____

T _____

I _____

O _____

N _____

Peer Pressure vs Peer Support

Write your own Scenario

Peer Pressure

_____

_____

_____

_____

_____

Peer Support

_____
_____
_____
_____
_____

Question:

Can Peer pressure ever be used for good?

_____
_____

How do you turn Peer pressure into Peer Support?

_____
_____

How do you show support to someone who needs it?

_____
_____

The Importance of Me time

1. How do you like to spend your Me time?

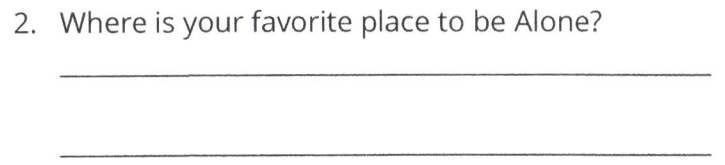

   _____
   _____

2. Where is your favorite place to be Alone?

   _____
   _____

3. Do you get "Do nothing self-care days? What do they look like

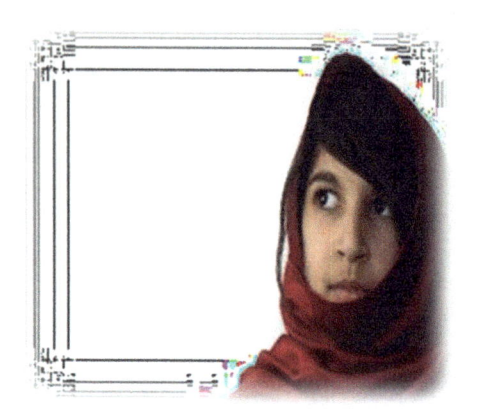

First, I _____

Then _____

Then _____

Then _____

Lastly _____

See a Need, Fill a Need

1. Who is someone you could help today? And how?

   _____
   _____
   _____
   _____

2. If you could invent something to help someone, what would it be?'

   _____
   _____
   _____

3. What is a skill you have that somebody needs?

   _____
   _____
   _____
   _____

Dream, Plan, Work, Earn

1. Do you Have a Goal for this Year? What is something you want

_____

_____

_____

_____

_____

2. How can you break your BIG GOAL into small steps?

Big Goal

_____
_____
_____

Step 1:
_____

Step 2:
_____

Step 3:
_____

Step 4:
_____

Step 5:
_____

Fill out the Goal Map

1. _____
2. _____
3. _____
4. _____
5. _____

Steps to My Goal

My Goal Is

Why do I want this goal?

When do I reach My Goal

What might stop me?

How do I get Past what might stop Me

Skills and Knowledge

What Do you know how to do?
1._____

2._____

3._____

What would you like to learn how to do?
1._____

2._____

3._____

Name a Book That you loved. What did you love about it?

_____

_____

_____

_____

_____

Who Is Your Favorite Teacher and Why?
_____

_____

_____

_____

_____

What is the most interesting thing you've ever learned?

_____

_____

_____

_____

_____

About The Author

Jasmine Henderson was born a " Military brat" on Eglin Airforce Base in Florida. This has resulted in her having 10 homes growing up, and 13 different schools.

Currently she lives in the Suburbs of Chicago with her teenage daughter. Jasmine attended North Carolina School of the Arts with a concentration in Production Design in Filmmaking.

Due to a diagnosis of Lupus Nephritis, she has had a rocky work history. Despite dialysis and two kidney transplants Jasmine has had various jobs. These experiences include a licensed CNA, Nanny, upholstery, and Licensed Barber.

She currently working at the public library.

In the past, Jasmine lead the kids praise team at her church until the children aged out. She also taught Youth church for the teens, heading several seasonal plays. This year she was the Arts and Crafts teacher for Church Camp.

Jasmine has spent time volunteering at the Tall Grass Art Gallery, and had the pleasure of curating one show " Graphics and Graffiti." She spent several years volunteering for the South Suburban Family Shelter.

Jasmine was inspired to write this book while running a "Girl Power" program at the library for girls 3rd - 6th grade, where they discussed themes like self-awareness and peer support, as well as building skills like goal mapping and budgeting.

Jasmine loves to create, be it drawing, knitting, or sculpting. She has had a love for books since she first learned to read, and she hopes to write more books someday.

Contact Jasmine

jlhenderson321@gmail.com

Photo Credit List

1. Pg 8 Credit: Tony Sharp

2. Pg 9 Credit: Muhammadtaha Ibrahim Ma'aji

3. Pg 11 Credit: Emiliano Vittoriosi

4. pg 13 Credit: Martin Bennie

5. pg 16 IStock:Staras

6. Pg 17 IStock - Credit:lzf

7. Pg 17 IStock Credit:yacobchuk

8. Pg 19 IStock - Credit:yacobchuk

9. Pg 22 IStock- Credit:jacoblund

10. Pg 26 -credit:Natalia Leb

11. Pg 27 – Credit Jasmine Henderson

12. Pg 30 - IStock - credit:dolgachov

13. Pg 33- Girl - Credit: diego_cervo

14. Pg. 36 -Credit IIONA VIRGIN

15. Pg 37 Prostock-Studio Stock photo ID:1342229939

16. Pg. 42 Credit Michelle Doykes

17. Pg. 48 Credit Arieliona

18. Pg. 50 Credit Honey Yanibel